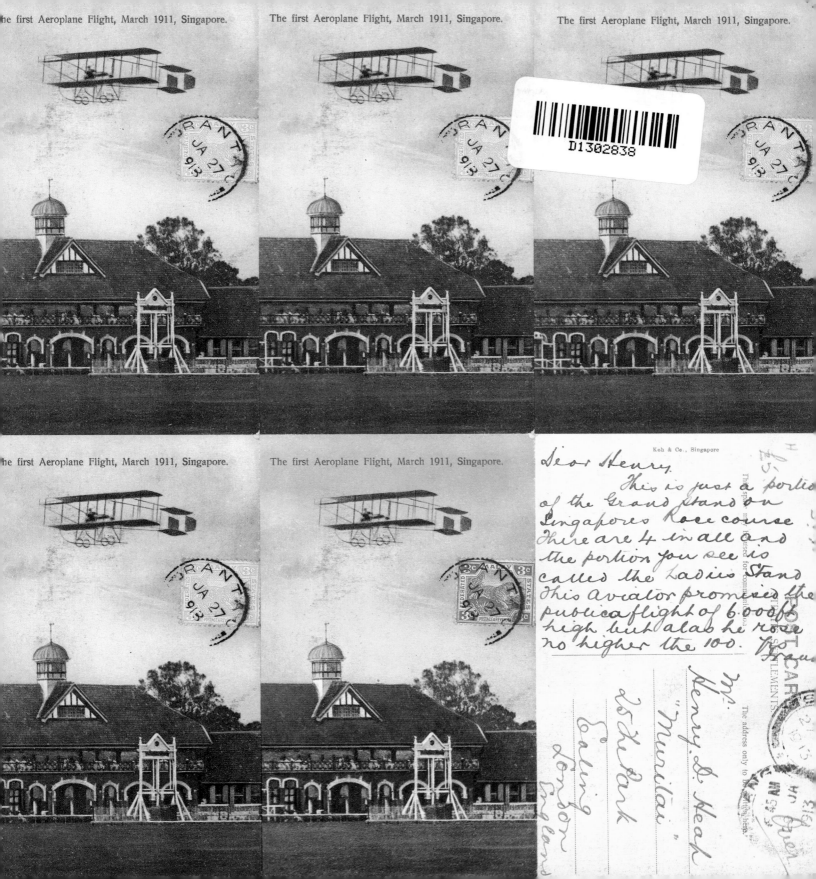

The first Aeroplane Flight, March 1911, Singapore.

Koh & Co., Singapore

Dear Henry,
This is just a portion of the Grand Stand on Singapore Race course. There are 4 in all and the portion you see is called the Ladies Stand. This Aviator promised the public a flight of 6.000 ft high but alas he rose no higher the 100.
Yours Frank

Mr.
Henry L. Heal,
"Munlai"
25 the Park
Ealing
London
England

POST CARD
FEDERATED MALAY STATES

SINGAPORE
from the air

IAN LLOYD · IRENE HOE

TIMES EDITIONS

Like a mirage from the past, an Indonesian trader sails past the ultra-modern backdrop of Tanjong Pagar container terminal and the city.

Overleaf: Many Singaporeans cherish hopes of a home by the sea or, at the very least, one with an ocean view but few are so privileged as those who live in the public housing apartments towering over East Coast Parkway — where re-sales can net five times the original cost.

CONTENTS

Singapore is a rough diamond 42 km by 23 km between longitudes 103° 38'E and 104° 06'E. The 570 sq km main island misses the equator by about 137 km, lying as it does between 1° 09'N and 1° 29'N. The coastline of about 132 km has had many of its original kinks ironed out and neatened by reclamation. The total land area of the island, and its more than 50 islets, comes to just over 625 sq km ...with nearly half already built up.

This is hardly surprising since Singapore held more than 4,200 persons per sq km by the late 1980s. The impression of people living on top of each other is made even more forcible when one considers that the population density is actually far greater — in excess of 7,500 per sq km — if uninhabited areas like forest, marshes, tidal wastes and other spaces which are virtually unpeopled — like inland waters, quarries and plantations — are excluded.

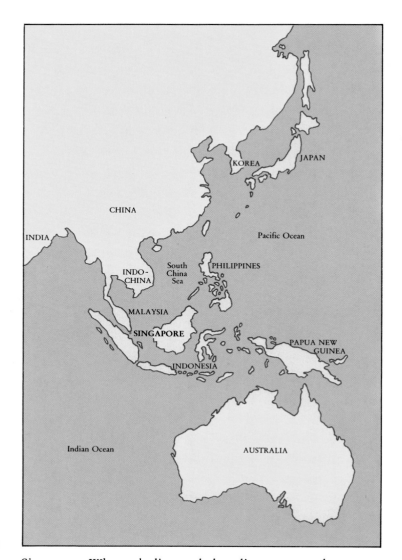

NATION CHANGING

Singapore. Where skyline and shoreline are remade year to year. Where mere months can turn calm countryside into clubby condominiums, shoving suburbs headlong into city neighbourhoods at a frenetic pace seldom matched elsewhere.

Blink and another old building is no more. Close your eyes and yet another row of old shophouses vanishes. Blink again and brand new shopping centres, offices or apartment blocks come up in their place — like so many latter-day phoenixes rising from the ashes.

Not for nothing has the ubiquitous tower crane been dubbed the national bird of this island. It is a bird in a hurry, one that seldom seems to sleep, drawing its energy from the wattage that floods the numerous construction sites scarring the main island's 570 sq km.

Reclamation works constantly nudge the shoreline

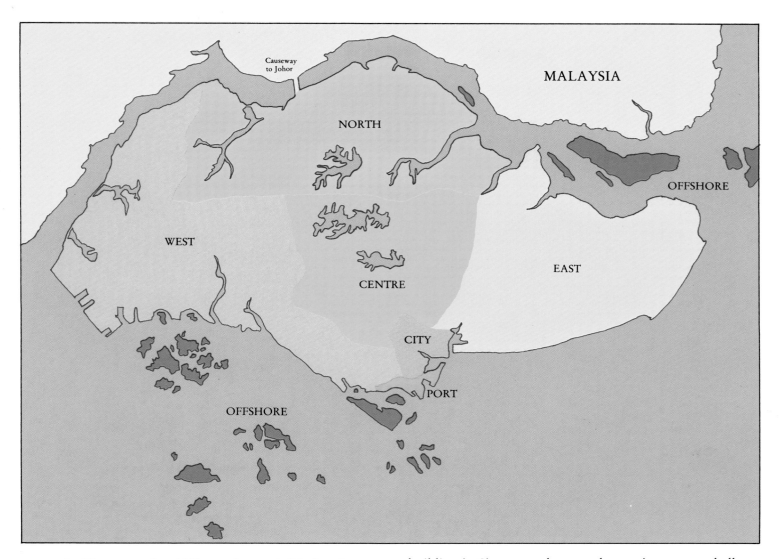

Causeway to Johor

MALAYSIA

NORTH

OFFSHORE

WEST

CENTRE

EAST

CITY

PORT

OFFSHORE

seawards, like so much middle-aged spread. Marina Centre, the sandy expanse lined with casuarina trees which lies south of the original city of Singapore, is all man-made. Like the massive East Coast Park, which stretches from just outside the city centre to Changi, it was once nothing but a gleam in a planner's eye.

The land area of Singapore and its offshore islands has grown to 625 sq km from 581 sq km in 1969, but on the way the country lost a few islands. In 1969 Singapore had 62 offshore islets. In 1989 it had just 57. Carelessness? No, reclamation. The missing islands have simply been merged with others nearby.

Ashore successive building booms extend reclamation heavenwards, jabbing the skyline with fingers of steel and concrete, gloved in tinted glass. No sooner has one manufactured monolith laid claim to being the tallest

building in Singapore than another springs up to challenge the record.

A key figure in the frenzy of construction is the country's biggest builder, the Housing and Development Board (HDB). Between 1960 and 1988 it had completed 620,467 dwellings — including one housing estate built entirely on reclaimed land. In the space of the five-year public housing plan, ending in 1990, it will have built 119,133 apartments, not to mention community centres, mosques, bus interchanges, swimming pools, sports complexes, industrial and commercial buildings, markets and food centres. Small wonder that by 1985 more than four out of five people in Singapore lived in homes built by the board.

The rest of the country lives — or so it would seem — on Orchard Road where a search for orchards is destined to be fruitless. Fruit trees are a rarity on this road which is hotel

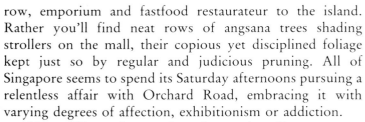

View of Singapore Town, Singapore.

Waterworks at foot of Gov. Hill. – Wasserwerk am Fusse des Gouverneurhügels. Singapore.

row, emporium and fastfood restaurateur to the island. Rather you'll find neat rows of angsana trees shading strollers on the mall, their copious yet disciplined foliage kept just so by regular and judicious pruning. All of Singapore seems to spend its Saturday afternoons pursuing a relentless affair with Orchard Road, embracing it with varying degrees of affection, exhibitionism or addiction.

How different it must have been when Singapore was the seaport of Tumasik (also known as Tan Ma-Hsi to its Chinese sojourners), founded in 1297 as one of the three kingdoms of the trading empire of Srivijaya based in Palembang in southern Sumatra, and destroyed in 1376 by the Java-based Majapahit empire.

When the founder of modern Singapore, Sir Thomas Stamford Raffles, first set foot ashore in 1819, greenery almost completely covered the island. Mangroves swamped

the right bank of the Singapore River, while native rhododendron and other shrubs colonised the opposite bank.

The river, now so neatly contained within concrete banks, then wound lazily through marshy islands as it neared the sea, barely pausing at the sandbar wedged in its mouth before spewing its contents into the Straits of Singapore.

Today Singapore is still surprisingly green, though it is often derided as a concrete jungle. The centre of the island is all vegetation and water because it is both forest reserve and catchment area, home to three major reservoirs. But there are fewer rivers now. Some, like the Kranji River in the northwestern corner of the island, have been dammed and turned into reservoirs.

Outside the nature reserves the greening of Singapore is careful and deliberate. Between 1981 and 1988 the records

5

7

THE HARBOUR, SINGAPORE

6

1. Fort Canning and its lighthouse presiding over Boat Quay around 1924.

2. Europeans played tennis on the Padang around the century's turn when this view was taken.

3. Panning further right, the Municipal Building — now City Hall — circa 1930.

4. Government House — today's Istana — overlooking Bukit Timah Road circa 1900.

5. Anderson Bridge — showing here pre-1922 — was opened in 1910 so traffic could cross the Singapore River mouth.

6. On June 12, 1937, an airshow marked the opening of Singapore's first civil aerodrome, Kallang Airport.

7. In the late 1920s the General Post Office operated from the still-standing warehouses while Fullerton Building was being constructed.

show that the Parks and Recreation Department planted precisely 281,388 trees and 1,237,837 shrubs; not to mention 630,071 creepers, climbers and hedges which ensure that not even a city road is without a touch of greenery for more than a short stretch of road being laid or widened. Within weeks one may expect to see the newly-planted stumps of what Singaporeans call "instant" trees sprouting their first tentative leaves to soften traffic islands and road dividers.

"The island of Singapore consists of a multitude of small hills," wrote naturalist Alfred Russel Wallace in 1869, just 50 years after Raffles arrived. It is a lot flatter now. Generations of builders have lopped and cropped hills to fill in swamps and to reclaim land from the sea.

Physically the island divides into three parts — the central hilly area from which protrude Bukit Timah, Bukit Gombak, Bukit Panjang and Bukit Mandai; a succession of

hills and valleys which undulates westwards; and a fairly flat plain of sand and gravel stretching from Katong to the easternmost tip, Changi.

Raffles, who wasted no time in hoisting the Union Jack over the island, began almost immediately to change the shape of his new colony. And the urge to reclaim has persisted to this day. First the Singapore River's north bank was drained and set aside for government buildings. Then in 1822 a hill where Raffles Square now stands was dug up and dumped on the south bank to form Boat Quay, now marked by the 40-storey headquarters of the United Overseas Bank.

In due course Mount Wallich, Bukit Kramat, Mount Palmer, Bain's Hill and others also gave up the ghost while names like Green Hill, Guthrie's Hill, Line Hill, Lessuden, Mount Harriet, Mount Victoria, Mount Zion and Rosemary's Hill slid into oblivion. Others were more fortunate.

Pearl's Hill only lost its head. Once cone-shaped, it had its crest chopped off when Fort Canning was built on the rise which still bears this name. The reason here was military but the result was the same.

Even Singapore's loftiest peak, 175-metre high Bukit Timah which means Tin Hill, is not immune to the depredations of development. A working quarry nibbles away at the hill which is solid granite under its jungle.

Covered as it is with tropical rainforest, Bukit Timah does not offer a great view. A better one must have been enjoyed by Mr P.H. Hilbourne, to whom the honour of being the first person to see Singapore from the air should probably go. Of course, Mr Hilbourne may have been too busy tending his hot-air balloon on the way up — and worrying where he should land on the way down — to admire the view on that historic day in 1910.

A year later a French airman, Joseph Christiaens, became the second person to enjoy an airborne perspective of Singapore. He made his ascent in a Bristol bi-plane which he had shipped to Singapore and assembled for the demonstration. Christiaens, who took off from the European Race Course, now Farrer Park, hardly skimmed the tree tops on his first try which took him not much higher than 10 metres off the ground. His best effort then — nearly 152 metres according to a newspaper report — would not have cleared Bukit Timah.

On a clear day you may just be able to see the whole island from the window seat of an airplane as it prepares to land at Changi Airport. Or better still, study the wrap-around panorama from the lofty crown of Raffles City's Westin Stamford hotel 73-storeys up. You'll see that Singapore takes its nation-building literally.

The seafront along the Esplanade had not yet been turned into a park when this photograph was taken between the end of the Second World War, in 1945, and the early 1950s. People have been taking the air on the Padang since the mid-1800s when the far corner, known as Scandal Point, was the evening venue for Europeans to gather, probably for a good gossip as the name suggests. As the photograph, above left, shows, today the Esplanade has lost its seafront to massive reclamation for Marina Centre.

Right and overleaf: In these aerial panoramas, taken in 1959, Asia Building still reigns as the country's tallest building: the fields of Shenton Way have not yet been claimed as car parks but Singapore Polytechnic — opened in 1959 — stands low-rise and white, facing the fields. In today's scene Asia Building is dwarfed by surrounding office towers.

Looking up and down river in the Sixties and Seventies the aerial view was dominated by bumboats, either moored along the quays in pleasing patterns, or puttering out to sea to ply cargoes between riverside warehouses and cargo ships at anchor. Today the bumboats cluster at sea at Pasir Panjang and the river patiently awaits a new *raison d'etre*. The older view, left, shows where Chinatown began, southwest of the river. Chinese immigrants were quick to stake claim to the land around the sea now known as Raffles Place and 22 of the original 51 titles for landed property went to pioneers of the different dialect groups.

Before the city shakes off the morning mist, its skyline might be that of almost any metropolis hooked on highrises but for the angular "hat" atop High Street Centre, next to the dome of the Supreme Court, the clock tower of the Victoria Memorial Hall and, just missing sunlight, the pointed tip of Asia Building.

Overleaf: Before the 1970s Shenton Way was better known for its parking lots which made a nightly transformation into a food centre, indulging the local penchant for midnight suppers.

Page 21: In the early years of public housing it was thought that most people would live in the city proper — all in housing estates no further than a 80¢ bus ride from each other. Bus fares aren't what they used to be, but people still prefer to live in proximity to the city. Public housing in this prime area is reserved for those whose homes are acquired by government.

'HEARTS' AND SOULS

CITY

The city has many hearts but no downtown to call its own. Its character owes much to Raffles' decision to keep the different communities separate — the better to keep the peace between them — through a town plan which reserved the area around the river mouth as well as the flats on its left bank for the cantonment and government buildings, housed the Europeans east of the cantonment, and settled the Chinese on the river's right bank.

Raffles' plan also called for Temenggong Abdu'r-Rahman, who controlled Johor, Singapore and neighbouring islands, and his people to settle in the area "from the site of the large bridge (now Elgin Bridge) up to the river towards the source".

Singapore's colonial heart, still home to many important functions of government, survives to stare down the skyscrapers it keeps at an aristocratic arm's length.

Modern Singapore was born on the lush stretch of green turf called the Padang (Malay for field) which faces the sea. If Singapore had crown jewels the Padang, once known as the Plain, would be its prize emerald, a national treasure permanently and unabashedly on show. No keeping off the grass here. From the most riotous of rugby games to the brass-band pomp and chest-thumping patriotism of National Day parades, the Padang has seen it all.

The field and its seafront made up the Esplanade which continues to be a popular promenade, though reclamation has pushed the sea so far back that it's hard to believe now that one could once catch sand crabs by just lowering a string over the railing to the sloping sea wall.

The Padang is history itself, surrounded by the colonial romance of landmarks including the Cricket Club (where the Europeans played cricket) and the Recreation Club (where the Eurasians played cricket) anchoring the west and east ends of the Padang, and City Hall and the Supreme Court lying along its length. They still play cricket at the clubs but several of the other buildings have been thoughtfully recycled. Parliament sits at the old Court House and what used to be the Town Hall is now home to the Singapore Symphony Orchestra, a theatre and a bank.

Next door the Sindhis, Gujaratis and Sikhs came off the boats that brought them from India and moved into High Street behind the colonial offices. They set up their clothing shops on this strip, which was later to become the place to buy one's linens, silks, satins and laces, until the 1970s when polyester and shopping at Orchard Road sent High Street into a tailspin from which it has yet to recover.

Most visitors seldom venture far from Orchard Road. It's easy to be Rip Van Winkle here. One need only nap for a

few years, perhaps mere months, to awake disorientated on this strip which was, till the turn of the century, a countryside where nutmeg trees formed whole plantations.

Another heart flourished on the other side of the river. Raffles Place was once the business centre. Every bank of consequence had to have its office in Commercial Square, as it was once called. It was developed in 1823-24 on Raffles' own orders. A small hill between Battery Road and the Square was removed, and the swamps drained, filled in and levelled, and later asphalted, concreted and tiled as well. In the late 1960s and 1970s, banks began shuffling westwards to Shenton Way, touted then as Singapore's answer to Wall Street.

The migration may have been hastened by a disastrous fire at what was then the country's premier department store, Robinson's, which appeared to signal the end of the

square's glory. But the bankers returned to newer high-rise prestige addresses which became available at the square in the 1980s. At least half a dozen major banks are headquartered on, or at least near, the square to the west of which the earliest Indian immigrants, including money lenders and small shopkeepers, set up their businesses.

Continuing renewal in the city has usually been at the expense of its old buildings. The face of the waterfront has gone through more than plaster surgery and several of the familiar buildings that greeted those arriving at Clifford Pier as late as the 1960s are no more. And those which linger on tend to be overshadowed by new, sleeker arrivals. The 1910 Alkaff Building, commonly known as The Arcade, has been replaced by a modern Arcade of shops and offices. And the glass-faced Ocean Building to its west is the third of that name on this site. One prominent survivor is Fullerton

Building, a massive grey block which still houses the General Post Office and other government offices.

Urban renewal has also eaten into the city's Chinese heart whose dilapidated rows of shophouses have steadily succumbed, like slow dominoes, to the wreckers' ball.

Chinatown was always a divided heart as Raffles believed in segregating not only races but also provincial groups. But somehow, though the Hokkiens have always been in the majority, it is the Cantonese influence that has weathered change, a flavour that lingers in its restaurants and in the market and food stalls now housed in the towering Chinatown Complex. The aroma of food is almost palpable. One never thinks of Chinatown without thinking of food. Hot chestnuts, peanut sweets, barbecued dried pork, turtle soup and herbal tea seem to lose something in translation when not eaten on a Chinatown street.

The old landmarks that endure are best appreciated at street level, for it is their detail rather than their form that sets them apart. The Thong Chai Medical Institution, set up in 1867 to provide free medical treatment to poor people of any race, survives as one of the country's 19 historic buildings gazetted as national monuments.

Not yet a national monument, though already an international shrine, is the Raffles Hotel whose near neighbour is towering Raffles City. Raffles Hotel, redolent of Kiplingesque memories, sits along the old seafront, once a fashionable neighbourhood. Raffles City rises from the rubble of the Raffles Institution. Their juxtaposition — one gently grounded in a whitewashed romantic past, the other pushing determinedly upwards in an aluminium-clad future — is symbolic of the development dilemma that confronts planners bred to believe the only way to go is up.

Raffles Place, originally named Commercial Square, centre of Singapore's business district, was given a new focus with the completion of an MRT (Mass Rapid Transit) station, part of an underground rail link between downtown and the suburbs.

The skyscrapers of Shenton Way, Singapore's "Wall Street", seen here from across Marina Bay, loom over the colonnades of the General Post Office. The 1950s ordinance limiting new buildings to 10-stories did not survive the property booms of the 1970s.

The highrise skyline seems to be advancing on Chinatown's pre-war shophouses, for which tenants and layers of sub-tenants pay rock-bottom controlled rentals — possibly the last true bargains in Singapore — to mainly absentee landlords.

Right: Spontaneous and tenacious hanging gardens of "strangling fig" sprout from the roofs and walls of Tanjong Pagar's shophouses.

Far right: A blur of trishaws whizz by bearing tourists through Chinatown's Temple Street where stalls like these once flowered every night. The stalls were moved indoors in 1983, most of them settling into the Chinatown Complex on Smith Street.

Chinatown celebrates the new year with a street show starring more than 600 lanterns, 90 street banners and 1,200 stalks of pussywillow put up by the Singapore Tourist Promotion Board when it lit up Chinatown for Chinese New Year the first time in 1985.

Right: Four troupes "chase the dragon" in the Chingay parade, staged on the first Sunday following the start of the lunar new year. The annual parade, which used to be held in housing estates, now packs them in at Orchard Road, the main artery of shopping.

Overleaf: As dusk approaches, the city explodes in a riot of lights. Along the waterfront, office blocks stand cheek by jowl in a show of fraternal display. But at 280 metres, the OUB Centre, left, towers over the rest, claiming its rightful place as Singapore's tallest building.

On Beach Road, a memorial built in 1967 by the Singapore Chinese Chamber of Commerce honours civilians who died during the Japanese Occupation of Singapore between 1942 and 1945.

Right: Air Force jets leave a pink trail over the 1984 National Day parade on the Padang, the city's best-known landmark and its largest green lung which is a popular venue for cricket, lawn tennis, field hockey and rugby.

Raffles and Raffles. When the Raffles Hotel opened on Beach Road in 1889 it looked out to sea until land reclamation, and new building, blocked the view. Those who stay in the towers of Raffles City's soaring hotels, particularly the 73-storey Westin Stamford, enjoy spectacular panoramas.

The Golden Mile lines up along Nicoll Highway, starting from the Plaza Hotel and its apartment tower at far left, to the Golden Mile Complex and the Woh Hup Complex whose terraced apartments were among the first modern buildings in this area.

The minarets of Sultan Mosque
are deliberately echoed in
the nearby Golden Landmark
building, designed as a centre
for jewellers in the Kampong
Glam area whose streets
were laid out as early as the
1830s. The yellow-ochre
building to the right of the
mosque is the Istana Kampong
Glam, built circa 1840
for Sultan Hussein Shah.

The open ground where the old
Fort Canning once stood
makes the site look particularly
defenceless in this view of
the hill looking towards
Orchard Road. Today the
chief attractions of Fort
Canning are the squash courts
and seafood restaurant housed
in a low, white-washed
building on the right.

Overleaf: Once likened at the
turn-of-the-century to "the
well-shaded avenue to an
English mansion", Orchard
Road meets Scotts Road
at what is probably the busiest
and most cosmopolitan
junction in Singapore.
Its landmark is the
pagoda-like tower of
the Dynasty Hotel,
one of the many hotels
completed in the hotel
building boom of
the early 1980s.

The chief breadwinner of the Port of Singapore Authority is the Tanjong Pagar Container Terminal, which handles 95 percent of the containers shipped in and out of Singapore. Its nine berths, served by 18 quay cranes, turn ships around in about eight hours on average.

Overleaf: Cruise ships tie up at this dedicated wharf near the World Trade Centre from which ferries, like the three seen berthed in front of it, carry visitors to the island of Sentosa. A second link, the cable car line, passes through PSA Towers to the left of the World Trade Centre. But it can barely be made out here as the system had not started up for the day when this photograph was taken shortly after sunrise. Keppel Shipyard, stretching across the rest of the frontage, was named after Admiral Sir Henry Keppel who, as a mere captain in the mid-1850s, saw the potential of the port.

Page 47: An oil tanker moves out to sea with the help of tugs from the Port of Singapore Authority. Ships of more than 600 lines fly flags of virtually all maritime countries linking Singapore to about 300 ports.

ROADS OF COMMERCE

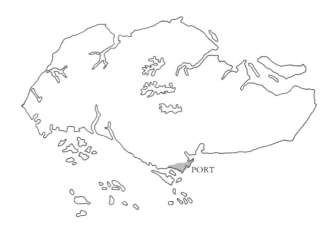

PORT

The world's second busiest harbour was known to sailors even in ancient times. The Chinese called it Lung-Ya-Men meaning Dragon Teeth Gate.

It had a most unsavoury reputation then. The first eye-witness description came from a 14th century Chinese trader, Wang Ta-Yuan, who portrayed the port of Tumasik as a place to dread. West-bound ships could pass safely *"but on the homeward run, junks put up padded screens as protection and prayed for fair winds to carry them safely past the savage Tan-ma-hsi, or Temasek pirates, who lurked in wait with as many as two or three hundred boats"* writes C. M. Turnbull in *A History of Singapore 1819-1975*.

Piracy was the last thing on the mind of Colonel William Farquhar, the first resident of Singapore, who was in ebullient mood when he wrote to Raffles in 1820:

"Nothing can possibly exceed the rising trade and general prosperity of this infant colony, indeed to look at our harbour just now, where upwards of twenty junks, three of which are from China, and two from Cochin China, the rest from Siam, and other vessels are at anchor, besides ships, brigs, etc. a person would naturally exclaim 'Surely this cannot be an establishment of only twenty months' standing.' One of the principal Chinese merchants told me, in the course of conversation, that he would be very glad to give $500,000 for the revenue of Singapore five years hence."

In 1822 139 square-rigged vessels and 1,434 native craft called at the port of Singapore in only its third year as a British trading post.

A scant seven years later came the first steamship to call at Singapore. Despite the advent of steamships, the roads continued to be filled with sailing ships for the next few decades. These had to lie with sails furled for weeks, sometimes months, for the next monsoon to arrive and blow them home or onward.

In 1845 the Peninsular & Oriental Steamship Company began monthly sailings to the Far East. Then, in 1855, P & O started sailing fortnightly from Europe. Singapore became a natural port of call between the sea-lanes which linked Europe with Australia, China and the rest of Asia. By the mid-1860s people complained if mail from England took longer than five weeks to reach Singapore, according to Turnbull.

Steamers raced ahead of sailing ships after the Suez Canal opened in 1869. As the steamships needed wharves, traffic dwindled in the roads where a typical day in 1865 used to see as many as 150 ships at anchor, and New Harbour became a scene of hectic activity.

New Harbour was renamed Keppel Harbour in 1900, after Admiral Sir Henry Keppel. But back in 1848, when he surveyed New Harbour and reported its advantages to the Admiralty, he was plain Captain Keppel. Though the Admiralty chose Hongkong over Singapore as its Far East naval headquarters, Keppel's faith in this island is remembered with some gratitude. He has a strait, an island, a road, a country club near the harbour and a shipyard named after him — more than some of Singapore's past governors.

The harbour had its beginnings in the Patent Slip and Dock Company, formed in 1861, which later became the New Harbour Dock Company. A rival Tanjong Pagar Dock Company was set up in 1864 and, despite some lean times, managed to acquire all its rivals including the New Harbour Dock Company in 1899. In 1905 it was taken over by the government, which is said to have paid out to the sharehol-

ders some $29 million for the port whose book value at the end of 1983 came to $1.3 billion.

As early as 1903, Singapore was already the world's seventh largest port in terms of shipping tonnage. In 1907, when a second edition of Reverend G. M. Reith's 1892 *Handbook to Singapore* was published, the Tanjong Pagar Dock Board had *"wharves a mile and a quarter in length, lying to the southwest of the city with which they are connected by electric tramways"*. It also owned two large Graving Docks, the 137 metre long Victoria Dock and the 145 metre long Albert Dock.

Large and well-fitted machine shops contained all that was needed for the rapid refitting of ships. There were also extensive godowns for receiving and storing cargo; and just behind the wharves, coal sheds which could hold 100,000 tons of coal. *"Ships are coaled by Chinese coolies with an*

astonishing rapidity," noted the handbook, whose writer would have been even more astonished to know that in 1985, according to some authorities, Singapore had become the world's largest port.

It was here that a Chinese coolie smoking in an attap-roofed coal shed set off a huge fire in 1877. The fire lasted for nearly a month, defying all attempts to extinguish it. By the time it burnt itself out it had gone through 50,000 tons of coal.

The Tanjong Pagar Dock Board later became the Singapore Harbour Board, the precursor of the Port of Singapore Authority (PSA) which was established on April 1, 1964. The Port of Singapore Authority runs Keppel, Pasir Panjang and Sembawang Wharves, Jurong Port and the Tanjong Pagar Container Terminal. By 1988 it was handling more than 390 million tonnes of freight, nearly 51 million

tonnes of it through the container of terminal — whose massive canary-yellow loading cranes seem to have been swiped from a Star Wars sound stage. From a distance the cranes' effortless loading of ribbed metal containers — like so many colourful building blocks — onto the ships, resembles robots with a Lego set.

How different from the scene that greeted surveyor John Turnbull Thomson in 1838, when he first set eyes on Singapore.

"*In the foreground, busy canoes, sampans, and tong-kangs bore their noisy and laughing native crews about the harbour. The stately 'Hyacinth' showed the pennant amongst numbers of English merchantmen. Hundreds of Chinese junks, and Malay prows, lay further inshore. Behind these, stretch a sandy beach, glistening in the sun, and overhung by the graceful plam trees, the glory of Singapore planters.*"

Previous page: The port records more than 60,000 arrivals and departures a year through its five gateways, the Tanjong Pagar Container Terminal (just visible in the upper right corner), Jurong Port and the Keppel, Sembawang and Pasir Panjang Wharves. Behind these ships, like Atlantis rising from the depths, the city skyline appears less-than-real behind Sentosa through the morning mist.

A semi-submersible oil rig waits at the long-term anchorage off west Jurong, which is also used by laid-up vessels. The ship in the distance marks the limits of the port. Beyond it is Indonesia's Pulau Karimun.

Right: In the days when *entrepôt* trade was Singapore's lifeblood, these bumboats played an indispensable role, ferrying cargo between ships anchored in the roads and the boat quays on the Singapore River. They were also pet subjects not only for tourists and amateur photographers but also for the legions of riverside artists who captured them in a thoroughly appropriate medium — water-colour.

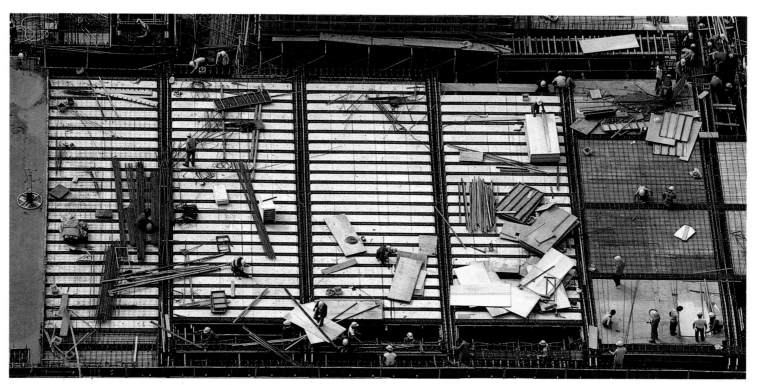

The quay crane is one of a new generation of port workers — yard gantry cranes, van carriers, prime movers, chassis and forklifts which shift about 20 million tonnes of cargo a year.

Above: Shipbuilding and ship repairing, a natural outgrowth of port activity, have gone on since the early years of modern Singapore. Between 1823 and the late 1860s boat-building and boat-repairing were carried out from Hallpike Boatyard on the Singapore River. Some of the modest yards which grew up in the Kallang Basin still survive many of the modern giants.

Singapore River lighters tie up at their new home near what is popularly known as Rat Island, off Pasir Panjang. But they don't make 'em like they used to anymore and the two bright yellow boats at the upper right corner are proof of this. The new-style bumboats have metal bodies.

Overleaf: Post-modernism struck quiet Pasir Panjang with a vengeance in the 1980s. While most of the new developments which sprouted along the island's west coast were fairly conventional in design, this quickly won itself the sobriquet of the Pink Ice-cream, melting down the slope in equal parts of pink and glass.

Page 57: From the air, trees moderate the quaint garishness of the figures and "rockscapes" which inhabit Haw Par Villa. The painted plaster park, also known as the Tiger Balm Gardens, was founded by the philanthropic Aw family which made its fortune from Tiger Balm ointment — commemorated by the three cheerful tigers located at lower left.

PAST LINKS TO FUTURE

WEST

Hell waits in the west. But its fires are so mellow you can go there and live to tell the tale. Haw Par Villa is home to the ten courts of Hades where the ghastly hereafter is depicted graphically in a medium which can only be called plaster grotesque. Justice does not equivocate here. Punishment is meted out to the unfilial, the untruthful, the unfaithful, the mendacious and their ilk, all portrayed in the lurid colour that pervades Disneyland East.

Haw Par Villa's neighbours were once seaside homes for the well-to-do. Some of the buildings still stand but they no longer snuggle by the sea, estranged by reclamation. Here and there family bungalows have given way to condominium highrises which hug the former shoreline of Pasir Panjang and climb its slopes.

Pasir Panjang, which translates literally as "long sand", was once predominantly a Malay area. Displaced by

expanding shipping and business interests from an earlier settlement at Telok Blangah to its east, the Malays had moved westwards along the coast with the boats and fishing nets from which they made a livelihood.

Now the vessels most evident along the West Coast are ocean-going ships which come alongside at the Pasir Panjang wharves to discharge cargo, and the sturdy — if inelegant — lighters which used to ply the Singapore River. The lighters are scant reminders of the past. The west is emphatically dedicated to a future with technology and tertiary education standing with arms linked. Set back from Pasir Panjang are undulating green slopes whose twisting curves once outlined a punishing course for the Gap Hill Climb, now just a fond memory for motor racers.

Placid green surrounds the Science Park, an industrial zone reserved for advanced technology which flows into the disciplined 150 hectare sprawl containing the National University of Singapore and its hospital on Kent Ridge. This region is home to two polytechnics and the university's sister school, Nanyang Technological Institute, farther west, whose Chinese-style sunken gardens are a reminder of the days when it won renown as the university of the south seas — Nanyang University. Now it houses thousands of engineering students and snuggles to its bosom an exquisite museum-quality collection of Chinese ceramics – as if to remind itself of its roots.

The Chinese Garden of Jurong echoes similar sentiments in traditional pagodas, arches and moongates. Seen through nature's soft-focus lens of early morning mist rising from Jurong Lake, the gardens provide a passable illusion of the Middle Kingdom. Sunday mid-morning finds the garden transformed into an outdoor bridal salon as white lace veils

and trains float over the lawns in hot pursuit of a definitively starry-eyed pose in front of a definitively scenic backdrop.

The softness of the gardens yields to more contemporary expressions assembled in concrete. Jurong's futuristic outcroppings rise like a badly-hewn Stonehenge. Sunset softens the harsh profiles of its characteristic city hall, the Science Centre and Unity House. The architecture is nothing to write home about but no VIP's trip is complete without a visit to Jurong, the largest industrial estate in the country and the prized showpiece of the Economic Development Board. Now they call it the "industrial miracle tour". But in the early days more spoke of Jurong as Goh's Folly — snidely named for the minister whose brainchild it was.

One lasting impression of Jurong that lives in the minds of those who don't live there is that it is far away. The new expressways make a nonsense of this prejudice but images of

Jurong's pioneering days, at the end of long, dusty roads petering off into sudden tracks, persist in the imagination, much to the annoyance of new-town residents who are at pains to tell you how civilised the far west really is.

At one end of Jurong the swampland that was Tuas evolved into a squatter settlement through no grand design. An old resident recalled how, in the mornings, it was not unusual to see 200 boats filled with fish. It seemed the most natural thing in the world for seafood shacks to spring up to take advantage of the catch landed there. But in the 1970s the huts began coming down as villagers started to be resettled in public housing estates, though the restaurants, unlike those which trade at Seafood Row on the East Coast, have maintained a somewhat steamier and seedier aura.

Tuas still spells seafood as it has for decades. A once-thriving fishing village of 10,000 people, and one of the last

56

on stilts, it needed no gimmicks to attract and all the advertising that was needed was done by word of mouth. While some diehard seafood lovers swore by Bedok, as many would swear by Tuas whose rough and ready wooden tables and chairs, with service to match, only seemed to add to its unpolished charms. With little ceremony, an enamel bowl half filled with hot water, a full teapot, bowls, small plates, sauce dishes and chopsticks would be deposited on the table with a clatter. With scarcely more reverence, the food would follow. Chilli crab. Mussels in chilli sauce. Steamed prawns. Tiny squid, crunchy crisp. Little hills of crab, prawn and mussel shells mounting in the semi-silence of absorbed eating.

A matching fascination for seafood pulses through Jurong Fishing Port in the early hours of the morning when the mainly Thai fishing vessels unload at the wholesale market. Restaurateurs and fishmongers aren't the only ones interested in the catch. Often, on a Saturday night, you'll find seafood lovers with pails and plastic bags in hand, sniffing out the lobsters, giant prawns, crayfish and table-size garoupas, snappers and pomfrets. There aren't many bargains to be had as the wholesalers are well aware of prices in town, but Singaporeans are sticklers for freshness in their seafood — never mind that on returning home much of their catch may well go straight into the freezer.

But these are pleasures not characteristic of Jurong whose attractions are the result of considered blueprints.

The planned naturalness of its Garden of Fame, where VIPs are invited to plant trees, the towering man-made waterfall in the Jurong Bird Park, Chinese and Japanese Gardens and country club golf course only serve to remind you that Jurong is, above all, a manufactured miracle.

Part of the Asian golf circuit, the Singapore Ladies' Open Golf Championship was played at the Jurong Country Club. A brash newcomer in the country club league, Jurong, which is popular with Japanese expatriates, raised eyebrows in 1984 when it boldly announced it was opening 20 corporate memberships at $140,000 which made its greens among the most expensive here.

Every Sunday is a wedding day at the Chinese Garden in Jurong whose 13 hectares were created in a $5 million manicure job. While bridal couples flock here in droves to be photographed at the stone boat, by the moongate, goldfish pond, at the pagodas and on the bridge, they weren't so keen on garden weddings and a special registry of marriage branch set up in mid-1982 closed after less than two years.

The design of public housing apartment blocks at Buona Vista, built in the mid-1970s, reveals their vintage through the wraparound corridors connecting all flats on the same storey. Four out of five Singaporeans live in the half a million apartments built by the Housing and Development Board in its first 25 years.

This is the place to get stuffed. Literally. Tanjong Penjuru is the location of this container stuffing and unstuffing yard through which many of the "boxes" — as the trade calls them — pass on their way to the Tanjong Pagar container terminal.

An unexpected taste of luxury on the Jurong River is provided by these Grand Banks cruisers — a faithful customer is Prince Bernhard of the Netherlands — made by American Marine.

The company, which is said to have built the first fibreglass boat ever made here, once sold the boat-loving prince a 50-footer with a price tag of more than a million dollars.

Two local supply craft refuel Thai fishing boats at the Jurong Fishing Port, one of the hottest "nightspots" in town where hardly anything happens before midnight and the action occurs on the floor in the early hours of the morning.

Overleaf: The lower bank of the Pandan River has all the makings of a superb traffic jam. In fact, you'd be hard put to find the crews manning these picturesque boats which bring in timber, rattan and bamboo from Indonesia.

Jack-up oil rigs wait for work in the waters off west Jurong, where other oil-related vessels are taking it easy at anchorage.

In the 1970s they couldn't build them fast enough, but by the mid-1980s new rigs were rarer than laid up ones.

No homes or industries lie within the boundaries of Upper Peirce Reservoir which is known as a protected catchment. It is among the older reservoirs and was opened to the public in 1979. Popular with birdwatchers, and also with joggers, the reservoir is out of bounds at night but this never seems to deter poachers.

Overleaf: The liberally sand-trapped golf course on the banks of the Lower Peirce Reservoir is part of the Singapore Island Country Club where "crab grass" is never so much as mentioned in polite company and lush greens go with plush membership fees in the six-figure league.

Page 71: First came the row houses in the centre, some of which have already aged into a second roof. Then came the apartment blocks of Ang Mo Kio. Now a third wave, this time a low-rise condominium development, in the foreground. These homes in the Yio Chu Kang area give a potted history of the homebuyer: the children, who grew up in the terrace houses, buy public housing apartments when they get married but aspire to give their children a stake in private property.

THE GOLDEN TRIANGLE

CENTRE

Condomania begins on the fringes of Orchard Road. Obligatory swimming pools squint into the sunlight as suntanned bodies dip into their plastic blue depths, embedded in practical plots of planned paradise.

While the brash newcomers tower upwards, the relatively aristocratic bungalows of old and new rich disdain the heights to sprawl nonchalantly over landscaped grounds in districts 9, 10 and 11. These are magic numbers in realtors' parlance, for this is the golden triangle of Singapore where homes with seven-digit price tags are no surprise and green baize lawns emanate an aura of money.

The fringes of the reservoirs are among the favourite haunts of birdwatchers who may be found, even before sun-up, stalking their prey with binoculars and notebooks in hand. Occasionally a seasoned member of the flock will attempt a birdcall, but on the whole they hunt in silence

seasoned with murmurs of delight, barely rustling the greenery.

Green is the true colour of the centre, but there is no price tag on the 75 hectares which make up the country's most valued natural treasure, the Bukit Timah (meaning "Tin Hill") nature reserve. From the air, or from the Pan Island Expressway, the canopy of dense green which crowns Singapore's highest topographical point at 175m is hardly impressive. But this treasure, the last bit of undisturbed primary rainforest in Singapore, is to be savoured quietly and from the inside.

The wealth of flora and fauna here is not measured by its flashiness but, like old money, its restraint. The forest boasts no birds with glorious splashes of colour. This would make them easy prey in the cool brown shadows cast by the towering dipterocarp trees — Singapore's answer to the giant redwoods of California. Close to the ground in Fern Valley are many delicate, diaphanous ferns only one cell thick and not to be found outside the forest. Only the occasional blast from the adjacent granite quarry reminds you that you are mere minutes from civilisation.

The centre has more than its fair share of greenery because it is also the island's main water catchment area with the MacRitchie, Lower and Upper Peirce Reservoirs set into secondary forest known locally as *belukar*, fringed by four golf courses all belonging to the Singapore Island Country Club.

The club was formed in 1963 by marrying the Singapore Golf Club to the Royal Island Club, a reluctant union which saw the "royal" label axed with such convenient dispatch that the regicide apparently escaped the notice of the newspaper columns. Even thus humbled, the club never pre-

tended to be ordinary and members paid — and continue to pay — for the *cachet* of belonging to the hangout of the rich and powerful. As far back as 1969 it moved a newsman to complain of the high cost of clubbing, noting how the club, which in 1965 cost non-golfers a mere $200 to join ($450 if you wanted to play), was charging $375 and $650 for new members four years later. One wonders what he would have said in 1983 when the club, whose lists are resolutely closed most of the time, offered 100 special corporate memberships at a cool $150,000 apiece! The greening of Singapore, indeed.

Green also inhabits the Singapore Turf Club, founded in 1842 and moved in 1933 to its present location along Bukit Timah Road in the prime residential area straddling the trunk roads north into the Causeway.

In the 1950s, recalls a long-time resident, there were only two dozen houses in Eng Neo Avenue which now

sweeps past the Turf Club to the expressway. It was like living in a jungle, with insects and snakes for company. Placidity still pervades the grounds during the week, but on weekends the aggressive traffic snarl of punters chokes the roads in a programmed annoyance homeowners have learned to live with.

South of "the turf", as regulars affectionately refer to it, the centre claims a disproportionate number of the Singapore's most prestigious schools, including many of its junior colleges and Christian mission schools, a sojourn in which is the closest thing to acquiring a domestic Ivy League pedigree. In their midst is the cradle of higher education once known as Raffles College. Over the years it has undergone intermediate metamorphoses so one might hear it variously referred to as the University of Malaya or the University of Singapore or, as its latest incarnation, the

Institute of Education which has as its backyard the Botanic Gardens, a popular haunt for joggers and *taiji* exponents and, at the end of its driveway, the A & W — Singapore's first drive-in restaurant.

This marks the start of Floral Mile, a length of nurseries lining the Bukit Timah canal which stubbornly resists all attempts at metrication. As children we would dare each other to cross the concrete arches that spanned the canal, adorned with barbed wire and iron spikes that enhanced, rather than diminished, its attraction for us. The brown water rippling down the canal was never as enticing, though it looks deceptively docile when it isn't its rainy day alter ego, a laterite-filled torrent churning downstream and overflowing to turn both the north and south trunk roads into one raging river. Once a man came paddling by in a boat during one of the periodic floods for which the area was famous. Despite flood-alleviation schemes, the canal still overflows, leading one exasperated drainage department official to say in 1980 that people would "just have to learn to live with the floods".

People have also learned to live with Toa Payoh, a swamp transformed into a prototype new town built under the country's second five-year public housing plan to provide homes for about 200,000 people. It has since become a fairly middle-income suburb, one of the few with a national monument to its name; the Siong Lim Temple, built between 1898 and 1908, is one of the largest Buddhist temples in Singapore.

It's hard to believe now that there was a time when Toa Payoh was raw and new. Yet Singaporeans once regarded the satellite town as though it was sited in outer space, just as the centre of the island was once nothing but plantations.

The double flyover which carries the north-south trunk roads — Bukit Timah and Dunearn roads — over a busy junction is one of more than 40 flyovers built here since the first was begun in the late 1960s. On rainy days north- and south-bound motorists have even more reason to be glad they can zip over this flood-prone intersection where Adam and Farrer roads meet.

From the air, Bukit Timah's patterns go from urban — like this mosaic of pale blue taxis and vivid blue, green, yellow vans and trucks — to a suburban crazy quilt of homes and gardens. But in the 1920's it was a tapestry of the greens of jungle and rubber estates dotted with small holdings where Chinese squatters grew fruit and vegetables.

Just waiting for a poolside barbecue, these dream homes of the 1980s, each house identifiably part of the group yet with a different identity down to the shape of the swimming pool, have one thing in common — they reek of money. Many older homes like the one in the background, which was probably built in colonial times, have added pools.

When land prices soared in the early 1980s, a new breed of luxury home emerged — the million dollar (or more) home in the sky for people who'd rather not be down-to-earth. One of these is a prominent landmark easily spotted from the Pan Island Expressway, known of course as the PIE.

The large terraces, tennis court and swimming pool at the bottom of the generous garden of this old house at Brizay Park, off Old Holland Road, seem designed for large, sporty families More contemporary homes, like those on the right, may still have swimming pools but are much more stingy with garden space.

Whatever the original purpose of the circular terrace, the owners of this house off old Sime Road, near the Singapore Island Country Club, clearly find it useful for airing laundry.

Overleaf: Every week 20,000 people visit the oldest public park in Singapore, the Botanic Gardens, founded in 1859. The gardens are especially well known for their orchid hybrids.

Sunlight and an evanescent morning mist transform Sembawang momentarily into a mysterious, almost spiritual celebration of dawn from the air. But the mist, not much more than moist breath, soon clears over the northernmost part of Singapore to reveal homes, shipyards and industrial buildings in what used to be the naval base from which Brittania ruled the waves in the Far East.

Overleaf: The heavily-silted waters of the Sembawang River deter all but the most determined of waterskiers, one of whom is seen making a turn on the river near a site nearly-cleared for industry.

Page 85: The muddy river suits these fishermen who are after prawns and small fish brought in by the tide. The device that looks like a wooden guillotine is actually a lock which is kept open for the incoming tide to sweep in the catch. Closed, it traps the prawns and fish inside the bund as the tide ebbs.

A RURAL VIEW

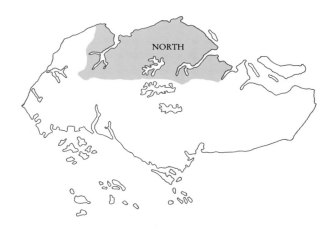

North lies the Causeway. Silvered pipes and a railroad track parallel a wide metalled road on this umbilical cord, of which Singapore's share is little more than half a kilometre long. Its lack of length belies the fact that it binds Singapore to Malaysia more securely and irrevocably than any political union.

Length for length, it is the most vital half kilometre for Singapore as well as the most symbolic of its dependence on the world outside. The Causeway moves food, water, people and more between the two countries, a ceaseless conduit of work and play kept in motion by half a dozen trains a day and staggering thousands of cars, buses, motor-cycles, scooters and lorries.

A traffic snarl on the Causeway is the surest indicator of a long weekend looming in Singapore. Locked onto automatic pilot, Singaporeans head north, the workaday rat race

translated into an aggressive mass migration of bumper-to-bumper cars elbowing their way towards the promise of weekend nirvana in Malaysia.

They are merely following in the tracks — figuratively if not literally — of travellers of old, obeying the same urge which led a Methodist Minister, G.M.Reith, to advise in a turn-of-the-century guidebook to Singapore:

"If the traveller have a little longer time, anything about five hours, he cannot do better than cross the island by the Singapore-Kranji Railway and thence to Johore. The Railway was opened in 1903, and before that, the trip to Johore was done by carriage, the road being a good one, and the journey giving an excellent idea of the interior of the island."

From there they would have had to swim — or take a boat to Johore. The Woodlands Road, even up to the early 1920s, ended at a bluff overlooking the insignificant railway station and the jetty for the Federated Malay States Railways passenger ferry to Johore Bahru where the real attraction then was a gambling farm, the licensed precursor of the gambling den.

That was when the Causeway was just a growing bund of granite rising from the Straits of Johore. When opened in September 1923, it was less than 20 metres wide and the Johore end featured a rolling lift bridge, unique in the Far East at that time, which allowed small craft to pass through the Straits — a boon now denied to the keelboat enthusiasts who, to compete in the annual round island race, must first take their boats to one side of the Causeway, then race all the way around to the other.

The Woodlands Road, before the Causeway opened, was still "a country road surfaced with laterite, so narrow beyond Bukit Timah that two vehicles could hardly pass",

according to a former newspaperman, George Peet. The factories which grew up along the trunk road leading from Bukit Timah were milestones which not only formed the meat of our lessons on local geography but also, when we were travelling "up country" by car, told us how far we'd progressed from town.

Tall apartment blocks have colonised Woodlands, which used to be little more than mangrove swamp and forest. But if there is one new town which has not lived up to its creators' ambitions it is Woodlands which was originally targeted, back in the mid-1960s, to be home to some quarter million souls by 1980. It continues to grow but it did miss its target spectacularly — by some 20,000 people. Town planners have allowed a few rubber trees and part of the mangrove swamp to remain to soften the contours of the landscaped lake garden in the housing estate which may yet grow up to be one of the prettiest because its creators have had a breathing space to work out some of the kinks in its making.

To the east lies Sembawang where Britannia once ruled the waves, its formerly formidable naval base now put to work as commercial shipyards and wharves, mainly for bulk cargo and timber, supervised by the national port authority.

More than a vestige of the military aura remains — Admiralty Road and Admiralty House are intact — but the uniformed presence is low-key as it is at Seletar which is a military airbase, aircraft maintenance centre, heliport and home to the local flying club as well as to the civilian families who rent houses once occupied by British forces.

Imperialism reigns here still. But quietly. And quietly too, a temperate climate governs the streets in the name of nostalgia. Piccadilly Circus is no raucous meeting place,

Regent Street offers no boutiques and you will look in vain for Speakers' Corner at Hyde Park, Seletar.

The north of Singapore is about as rural as you can get. Once the playground of crocodiles, the streams — nominally elevated to the status of rivers — are being domesticated into canals and reservoirs. Thus the Kranji River in the northwest corner has now become the Kranji Reservoir.

Even the farms have become citified. The odd chicken or duck still to be found scratching in the dirt is no inmate of the modern poultry farms of Choa Chu Kang. The pigs of Punggol now live in well-ventilated tin-roofed sheds, though the legacy of the time when they rooted in the open is still evident from the pungent aroma that rises from Punggol River, especially at low tide — one reason why even diehard waterskiers take to the water at high tide only. Despite the attempt to house these animals under more sanitary conditions, the problem of environmental pollution still persists, and this sector of the livestock industry no longer enjoys a favoured status in clean and green Singapore.

From the air, the north is astonishingly green. Much of this is forest which still covers nearly 30 sq km of the island. Neat vegetable gardens and small orchards still survive as a dwindling number of families work the land, till their turn comes to leave their rambling and familiarly ramshackle home for high-rise apartments in new towns like Ang Mo Kio, a paradigm of the Singapore good life.

Nor are the dead forgotten. At Kong Meng Sua — the Hokkien name for Bright Hill — where the Phor Kark See temple complex lives up to its name in a gaudy gilded sprawl, the ashes of the dead are housed in columbaria in rows of marble-fronted pigeonholes stacked high. The dead, too, moves upwards in Singapore.

Not to be found in any zoological tome is the paddle-wheeled weed eater, spotted here having breakfast on the Seletar Reservoir. The reservoir, completed in 1940 and extended in the late 1960s, is one of three set in the forests of the island's main water catchment area.

Lifelines for Singapore — water, rail and road — cross the Straits of Johore on the 1,056 m Causeway. When opened in 1923 it was less than 20 metres wide and a rolling lift bridge at the Johore end allowed small boats to pass through.

The onion-domed minaret of Masjid An-Nur, better known as the blue mosque, stands more than 21-storeys tall, a landmark visible from most parts of Woodlands new town — once planned to be the country's largest public housing estate, just a hop and skip from Johore Bahru. To the town's left is the immigration checkpoint, while in the foreground trees disguise a Malay village or *kampung*.

South of Woodlands new town, where a hill is being carted away by the truckload, a line forms as truck drivers, who are paid by the load, queue up to hand in their tally tickets.

At Woodlands East, the Jurong Town Corporation clears land for future industrial development. The corporation is one of the largest landlords in the country, managing more than 20 industrial estates.

Recreational fishponds, sometimes side by side with commercial ponds, have come back in a big way though most Singapore anglers still prefer the sea. The intrepid fishermen who step off the laterite track onto these treacherous carpets of bright green in Ulu Sembawang may find themselves splashing among the fish.

Orchids are a multi-million dollar export business for the country. More than $10 million worth of cut orchids are airfreighted to major cities around the world every year. Many come from Singapore Orchids' nurseries at Mandai. From the air, the neat rows and curves of its orchid beds resemble caterpillars sunbathing on the lawn.

Overleaf: In colonial times, the Admiralty housed its officers in this ring of homes off Admiralty Road West, now leased out by the government. The kitchen and servants' quarters were separated from the main house by a covered staircase and walkway — perhaps as a precaution against fire. Overhanging eaves and airy verandahs kept the houses cool.

The Chinese monopolised vegetable gardening in Singapore but farms now produce less than a quarter of the fresh vegetables that the country eats. Much of the market produce here is trucked in from Malaysia and airflown fruit and vegetables are common, if still expensive.

Farmland occupies only about 21 sq km of the island if plantations devoted to coconut and rubber are excluded. By the late 1980s there were only about 2,100 farms producing pigs, poultry, eggs, vegetables and fish, and their numbers continue to shrink. Green vegetables, including watercress and local varieties of lettuce and spinach, are popular crops for vegetable gardens like this one in Ulu Sembawang.

When the wind's up on a weekend, less-than-agile sunbathers are liable to get trampled as windsurfers hurtle seawards with their sailboards at the East Coast Sailing Centre, pictured here during a quieter moment mid-week. A savvy novice, the red sail of his trainer board just visible in the lagoon beyond the trees, tries out his sea-legs in the East Coast lagoon. The bright orange strip atop the apartment block is the Bedok lighthouse.

Overleaf: An expressway interchange flows over the East Coast Parkway, cutting a swathe through the Marine Parade housing estate, built entirely on reclaimed land, some of whose apartments command breezy panoramas and six-figured resale price tags.

Page 101: The Chinese Swimming Club with its two 50-metre swimming pools still straddles Amber Road as it did before but its beach of old, which began where the U-shaped three storey clubhouse ended, has moved south across the highway beyond the tennis courts. New highrises, many of them luxury condominiums, have put down roots in an area once noted for weekend homes for the wealthy.

SKYWARDS AND SEAWARDS

EAST

They don't fly kites on the East Coast anymore. The new toys that take to the skies over Changi Point — no strings attached — are sleek, silver-bodied airplanes.

This is Changi Airport, the business end of eastern Singapore and an inextricable part of this curious combination of business and pleasure. The airport is a Venus rising from a reclaimed sea, a city unto itself, with its own two reservoirs. It is a picture of efficiency, yet not without unconscious whimsy, especially at night when its control tower, so aloof in the sunlight, takes on a marked resemblance to an ice-cream sundae topped with a cherry, proffered, atop a 78-metre pole, to the gods of the skies.

When Sir Cecil Clementi said in 1931: "I expect to see Singapore become one of the largest and most important airports of the world" he wasn't of course thinking of Changi but of Kallang, Singapore's second civil airport,

opened officially in 1937. Instead of airplanes, basketball players now have the run of the concrete apron and the terminal building is headquarters of the People's Association, parent body of the island's community centres. Across the highway, megawattage lights the National Stadium on nights when it pays tribute to a minor national obsession — football.

The airport moved northeastwards in 1955 to Paya Lebar, near where the Japanese had once laid a wartime airstrip. The new airport began with a temporary terminal building, a shack which served as an air control centre, a fire station, two hangars and a Shell fuel farm. But it had a proper runway, not a turfed landing ground like Kallang. A new air traffic control centre, which began operating there in 1961, has seen many aviation milestones — its first jumbo jet, a B747, landed in 1971, and the supersonic Concorde

followed the next year, the same year Singapore Airlines flew solo.

In 1978 it could boast of the longest building in Southeast Asia — a new arrival hall whose days were numbered paradoxically even before it was completed as a generation-old dream of an airport at Changi — thought impossible in the mid-1940s — was revived, and a military airbase grew up to become an airport. It still stretches the imagination to think that there was once nothing but water where the passenger terminal building, cargo terminal and east runway now stand.

The Point still bears traces of its former career as a British airbase, though the airmen have long gone, leaving behind the pubs with the darts boards, now reformed into nightclubby restaurants which Changi Village wears like medals of undistinguished service. At nearby Loyang, the

future beckons from the centre of a burgeoning aerospace industry.

The beach endures, observing a constant ritual purification by wind and water. Crushed and obliterated by tonnes of sand and rock, ruthlessly reshaped and remodelled by reclamation, it somehow survives each successive seachange thrust upon it. The seaside bungalow was an icon of school holidays spent at "Brighton", "Clifton" or "Hove", named no doubt by some long-gone Briton seized by homesickness.

In bedrooms so large they seemed to echo, we children slept ten to a room — if we slept at all — while adults communed over mahjong spiced with gossip. At night, by torchlight, the older ones derived fiendish pleasure from terrifying the younger children with tales of headless ghosts stalking Tanah Merah (the name, "red earth", came from wartime massacres which bloodied the beach).

Changed beyond recognition from the picnic spot it has been since the 1850s, the Point manages to stay on familiar terms with weekend anglers, waders and those who come merely to watch the waves making obeisance to Neptune. The celebration goes on along a man-made fringe of sand which stretches to Sheares Bridge, a giant multi-tiered viaduct astride the Kallang estuary. From there you can spot a local landmark which, dwarfed as it is by all the newer buildings around it, would still be recognisable to those who were alive at the turn of the century. The Kallang Gasworks is an astonishing reassurance that some things don't change.

East of the Kallang River, many of the luxurious villas and bungalows of the moneyed Chinese families who built with weekends in mind on the seafront at Tanjong Rhu and Tanjong Katong, have given way to towering apartment blocks which dominate the view. The remaining beachside

mansions stand estranged from the once-intimate tides by an expressway and a broad casuarina-covered expanse of park, sad facades silently lamenting the loss of a private privilege to a playground gone public.

Before it became fashionable to build a seaside residence at Tanjong Katong, on the eastern fringe of the land originally ceded to the British, there was not much more than the beach, coconut trees and *attap* houses, until the Sea View Hotel, since rebuilt and rebuilt, was set up in the late 1800s in a grove of coconut palms on the seafront.

Near the hotel's multi-storeyed successor, the deep blue roof tiles of the new Chinese Swimming Club surround an Olympic-sized pool, duly chlorinated, where the old club used to have salt water in its swimming pools and also offered sea bathing in a fenced-in enclosure, or *pagar*, which kept the sharks out. More modern hazards dog watersports

these days. Windsurfers keep a keener eye out for oil tankers and barges than for sharks.

Home base for boardsailors is the East Coast Sailing Centre, also known as the Singapore Riviera — and occasionally as Riviera East — as much for its weekend complement of bronzed bodies and bikinis as for its popularity with the French community. Monsoon season finds the flotilla out in force, often braving the rain as well as gusty winds and waves. Even without gales, it's not uncommon for the rescue boat to be sent out to succour the intrepid and the unskilled who may suddenly find themselves half way to Indonesia.

By night, when the bathers and windsurfers have come ashore, and the anglers have reeled in their lines, the pleasuring continues under cover of darkness as East Coast Park gets on with the serious business of playing Cupid.

A pole vaulter makes a soft landing on a PVC-covered mattress at the sports complex in Kallang Park where once DC-2s and DC-3s touched down on a grassy circular landing area reclaimed from the Kallang Basin — the splashdown point for seaplanes at Kallang Airport, the country's first civil airport which closed in 1955.

Football is the name of the game at the National Stadium where capacity crowds have been known to bend their 60,000 sets of vocal chords to produce what locals call the "Kallang Roar" when the national football team plays.

Right: People regularly lose their way in the massive multi-level car park in one of the largest shopping centres, Parkway Parade, whose technicolour roof garden — actually a children's playground — overlooks the East Coast Parkway.

Becalmed windsurfers down sails and drown sorrows at the beach bar partly hidden by the large evergreen. Rows of zinc roofs provide shelter for members' boards while Hobie Cats and dinghies park in the open at the western end of the East Coast Sailing Centre.

Bumboats, launches, speedboats
and sampans crowd the small
jetty at the mouth of the
Changi River, from which
a casual ferry service operates
to the islands northeast of
Singapore which include
the two largest, Pulau
Tekong Besar and Pulau Ubin.

A throwback to earlier, lazier days, this Punggol bungalow, which belongs to a prominent Singaporean, is one of a disappearing breed raised above the ground on piers.

Right: A maze of unmarked tracks and potholed roads links homes in once-rural Loyang where the weekend homes of the rich were never far from the attap-and-zinc-roofed *kampung* houses of the villagers meagerly shaded by coconut palms. From this picture, little seems to have changed but only a short distance away is the centre of the country's burgeoning aerospace industry.

Sultan Shoal Lighthouse, at the western end of Singapore, is the youngest of its three offshore lighthouses. As the name suggests, it was once an underwater sandbank. Completed in 1896, the pile lighthouse, so called because it was built on concrete piles, turned a one-time shipping hazard into a boon to navigators but the island was only born after reclamation in 1975.

Overleaf: Pulau Setumu is the name of this island, 23 km south of Singapore, but most know it better as Raffles Lighthouse which guards the entrance to the Straits of Malacca. The light, more than 30 metres above high water, was first lit on December 1, 1855. In the background a VLCC, or Very Large Crude Carrier, enters the Straits on its return voyage.

Page 113: Off Pulau Ubin, in the northeast, the long arms of a *kelong* lure fish to large square nets where the catch is hauled up several times a day by fishermen who live in these traditional fish farms on stilts.

ISLAND IDYLLS

OFFSHORE

OFFSHORE

Treasure island. Pleasure island. Leisure island.

The idyllic offshore isle is an illusion nurtured by day-trippers who ferry soft drinks and sandwiches to a farther shoreline where, turning their backs to the minor tidal waves churned up by passing oil tankers, they drink to the ghosts of perfect picnics past in a weekend game of pretend.

The fading glory of the coral reefs fights a hopeless rearguard action against one of the busiest ports in the world and pillaging souvenir hunters who regularly come ashore at pleasure boat piers, staggering under their spoils of living coral.

No pellucid emerald green waters here now. Singapore's offshore islands wear the slightly muddied blue collars of the working class. Though they once owned a more leisured lifestyle, most have succumbed to the work ethic that drives

the entire country to ever-increasing economic goals.

Island life does have its high points — literally. Three of them to be precise: Singapore's lighthouses, the baby among them being Sultan Shoal Light. The senior citizen is Horsburgh Light which celebrated its centenary in 1951. Horsburgh, built on Pedra Branca which translates as "white rock", marks the eastern gateway to Singapore waters. The first granite lighthouse in this part of the world. The perfect whiteness of the rock, as more than one observer has noted, is due not to extreme purity but to the dung of seabirds that rest there! At the other end of the Singapore Straits, Raffles Light guards the outer and south channel round St John's Island to the Singapore roads, as it has since 1855.

The island people who once would come ashore to study and work, but return home to live, are coming ashore for good, adjusting their *kampung* dreams to highrise aspirations.

Pulau Bukom started work in 1892 and has yet to retire. As children we called it Shell Island, a name which has little to do with the seashell which is its corporate symbol and everything to do with the international oil company which still runs one of the largest refineries in the world on Bukom, originally a storage centre for kerosene.One end looks and lives much like a resort condominium, enviably complete with a country club for Shell employees who live on the island. The business end is an organised tangle of silvered tanks, boilers and pipes.

Unlike Bukom, Sentosa plays at being a resort. But the third largest offshore island earns its daily bread by harbouring a satellite earth station whose beeps and blips keep Singapore wired into the electronic grapevine of the rest of the world. Before its determined transformation into

a holiday and recreation spot, Sentosa, the Isle of Tranquillity, bore the deliciously romantic — if undeniably sinister — label of Pulau Blakang Mati which translates as "the island where death lies behind".

Pulau Brani, Island of the Brave, was once home to the Orang Laut, Singapore's sea gypsies whose sampan armadas treated passing boats as fair game. The island became a coaling station for British naval vessels and a small repair dock was built there in the 1860s. In 1890 the Straits Trading Company set up a tin smelter on the island, which also boasted Singapore's oldest football club. Brani, which used to be a 10-minute boat ride from Jardine Steps when the current was right — 20 minutes if it wasn't — is now home to the Republic of Singapore Navy.

Pilgrims to Pulau Kusu, 5.6 km from Singapore, now take its broad, manicured fringes for granted but the drawing power of its two shrines, a Chinese temple and a hilltop Muslim *kramat*, was such that there used to be barely wading room during the Kusu Festival in the ninth month of the lunar year.

It was easy to spot the genuine pilgrim. He was the tattooed youth in slippers, knee deep in water, bellbottom jeans nearly soaked to the waist, and in one hand a pink plastic bag with oranges and jossticks for the spirits and a packet of cigarettes for himself. She was the old lady, belongings securely zippered into a black tote bag, her black silk trousers pinned up perhaps with clothes pegs revealing smooth moon-pale legs.

Reclamation provided more standing room so, while pilgrims have, in a manner of speaking, dried up, there are more of them than ever.

At the rate it's reclaiming, Singapore will soon merge

with Indonesia, goes a local joke. The joke's gone a step further on Pulau Busing in the southwest. It will always be more Indonesian than Singaporean because its landfill comes from Indonesian shoals and islands.

Oil is definitely thicker than water in those islands southwest of Singapore which are well on their way to becoming a major international petroleum and petrochemical manufacturing centre. Creeping reclamation surreptitiously marries island to island, simultaneously wedded and welded by tonnes of sand which bury their former identities.

Islands get lost in other ways. You hardly hear the name Pulau Ayer Chawan used on the 169-hectare island which entered the 20th century as a carefree swamp and now works around the clock on three shifts, flying the Esso flag. Efficiency, and a penchant for acronyms amounting almost to an obssession, has cropped the name of Singapore's fifth largest isle, albeit unofficially, to PAC.

In time, no doubt, neighbouring Pulau Ayer Merbau, the site of a $2 billion petrochemical plant which started up in 1984, will be simply be referred to as PAM.

South of PAC lie Singapore's most tortured islands, Pawai, Sudong and Senang, where the jungle green you see is as much natural foliage as army camouflage for these are kept exclusively for military use.

The islands of the northeast are still cherished by the pleasure boats which zip food-lovers to a Sunday seafood restaurant with no name on the beaches of Pulau Ubin where the clientele is as casual and relaxed as the cooks who may take up to an hour to prepare a meal.

As if to make up for its vanishing islands, and those now off-limits to ordinary folk, Singapore is in the business of creating new islands from old coral reefs. Made in Singapore.

Floating fish farms like these lying off Changi Point (upper right corner) supply "live" seafood restaurants where one's dinner can be seen swimming about in tanks.

Right: A fish farmer's assistant sprays the timber decks with powerful jets of seawater after feeding the fish — seabass and garoupa are popular varieties — reared in nylon cage nets.

Tyre tracks mark
newly-reclaimed land on Pulau
Sakra/Bakau, once separate
islands south of the industrial
estate of Jurong, in a
multi-million dollar marriage
deal to increase the land area
tenfold to 155 hectares.

Top: Before three billion cubic metres of landfill from Indonesia merged these two patches of land, neither much more than reefs when this picture was taken, they could scarcely be called islands. Remade as Pulau Busing after more than a year of reclamation, which has created a 54-hectare island, this spot is the site of the country's second offshore oil terminal.

Above: Singapore has been perfecting the technology of reclamation since the early 1820s when swarms of migrant labourers shovelled away hills and made fill for Boat Quay and Raffles Place. Today offshore waters and islands provide the sand to re-shape Singapore and granite blocks to reinforce new contours from erosion by the sea.

Moongates and pagodas mark Pulau Kusu, or Tortoise Island, out from the others. Looking like a refugee from the Chinese Garden in Jurong, Kusu, nearly 6 km from Singapore, waits for the annual rush of pilgrims to its two shrines, a Muslim *kramat* on a hill which co-exists with a Chinese temple. A turtle pool, tortoise sanctuary and swimming lagoon do business year-round on this 8.5 hectare island.

People still don't lock their doors on Pulau Seking, whose lone policeman pounds his beat in 20 minutes flat. Seking, or Sakeng as it is also known, is to be joined to its larger neighbour Pulau Semakau to form a single 600-hectare island.

Once it bore the name Blakang Mati, or "Death Lurks Behind", but now Sentosa, "Isle of Tranquillity", lives up to its name in most parts except at this dread spot which has gained notoriety for lost balls.

The second hole of the Tanjong course, one of two run by the Sentosa Golf Club, is actually on a separate island joined to Sentosa by a bridge.

The island's preferred mode of transport is the monorail which takes ferry visitors to the island's only hotel, the swimming lagoon, cable-car station and the major sights on the island which include an old British fort and a maritime museum.

Above, right: Water cycles, pedal boats and skiffs wait for customers in the part of the island's man-made lagoon reserved for swimmers and slowpokes. Another part of the lagoon accommodates windsurfers and canoeists.

Above: Popular with loners and lovers alike, the lagoon is most tranquil on weekdays when one can almost be an island by monopolising the raft anchored mid-lagoon and fending off all boarders.

Overleaf: Traditional fisherfolk believe women bring bad luck to the *kelong* but this superstition rarely poses a problem now. As the catch dwindled some *kelongs* have been abandoned while others are rented out as occasional weekend retreats.

The first Aeroplane Flight, March 1911, Singapore.